I CAN BE A
RACE CAR DRIVER

By Sylvia Wilkinson

Prepared under the direction of Robert Hillerich, Ph.D.

CHILDRENS PRESS ®

CHICAGO

Library of Congress Cataloging-in-Publication Data
Wilkinson, Sylvia, 1940-
   I can be a race car driver.
   (I can be)
   Summary: Discusses the sport of race car driving
and the dangers of the occupation.
   1. Automobile racing—Juvenile literature.
   [1. Automobile racing—Vocational guidance.
2. Vocational guidance. 3. Occupations]
I. Title. II. Series.
GV1029.W4967   1986   796.7'2'023   86-9639
ISBN 0-516-01898-1

Childrens Press, Chicago
Copyright ©1986 by Regensteiner Publishing Enterprises, Inc.
All rights reserved. Published simultaneously in Canada.
Printed in the United States of America.
  4 5 6 7 8 9 10 R 95 94 93 92 91

PICTURE DICTIONARY

race car

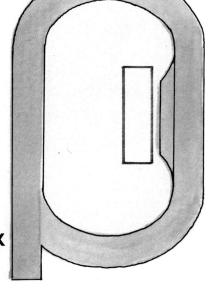

race track

kart

blowout

driver's license

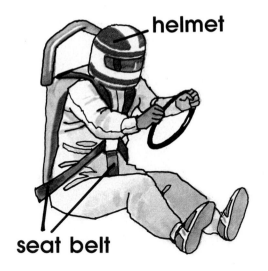

helmet

seat belt

racing team

race car driver

racing crew

pit

There are many different kinds, or classes, of race cars. But the drivers all have one thing in common—they like to go fast.

Do you like to go fast? Have you ever gone around a corner fast in your wagon, on your skateboard, or on your bicycle? Do you like to be the fastest in your neighborhood? Maybe you can be a race car driver.

race car driver

The race track at Watkins Glen, New York

race car

race track

Race car drivers drive race cars on special roads called race tracks. Some tracks are paved, like a highway. Some are dirt. Some go in a circle. Some go around curves and up and down hills.

Above: Racing on ice at Quebec's Winter Carnival
Below: The Montreal Grand Prix (left). Go-kart on a dirt track (right)

Weighing a go-kart before a race

kart

Race car drivers drive many different kinds of race cars. The smallest race car can be raced when the driver is only eight years old. It is called a kart or go-kart.

Racing go-karts

A kart goes around
turns very fast. It has four
wheels, a seat, and an
engine. The engine is
like the motor on a
lawnmower. Almost all
the famous race car
drivers first drove karts.

Left: Racer A. J. Foyt's car at the Indianapolis 500
Above: A Ford-powered Formula Atlantic car

driver's license

Race car drivers go to
school to learn to race
cars. When they are old
enough to have a
driver's license, they can
go to race driving
school. Here they learn
how to drive quickly

Racer Emerson Fittipaldi at the Long Beach, California, Grand Prix

through turns and
curves. They learn how to
pass other drivers. They
even learn how to stop.
One of the most
important things they
learn is how to drive fast
safely.

Accidents are a fact of life for racers.

Race car driving is very dangerous. Many people have accidents in regular cars on the highway. They are not going as fast as race car drivers. Race car drivers are better drivers than most other people, but they have accidents too.

blowout

They have accidents because they are going so fast. Sometimes they have accidents because parts on their cars break. They have blowouts. In a blowout, a large hole bursts in a tire and the air blows out. This often makes the car go out of control, hit a

Emergency workers help the driver out of a crashed race car.

wall, or turn over. If you
decide to make your
living as a race driver,
you must be prepared to
have accidents.

How do race drivers
protect their bodies in
an accident?

helmet

seat belt

The most important
item they wear is a
helmet. This covers the
head with a hard shell.
The helmet also has a
plastic cover in front that
the driver can see
through. This protects the
eyes.

Another important
safety item is the seat

Some of a race car driver's safety equipment: a helmet with a lift-up visor for eye protection; seat belts (blue straps); and roll bar (metal tube behind head), which protects the driver if the car should turn over

belt. Do you always buckle your seat belt when you ride in a car? Race drivers do. The

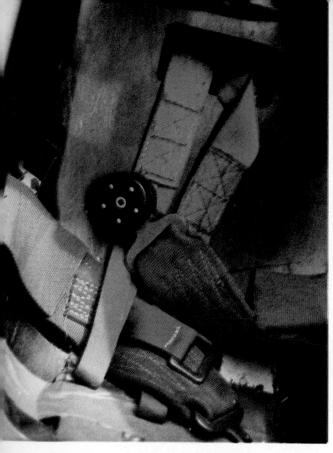

Left: Seat belts. Right: Fire-resistant suit and face mask

fastest race cars have
special seat belts that
hold the driver in the
seat from five
directions—two straps
over the shoulders, two
straps around the waist,

and one between the legs. All of these straps fit into one buckle so the driver can buckle up or unbuckle quickly.

Sometimes race cars crash and catch on fire. For this a driver wears a special suit, gloves, shoes, and long underwear. These clothes keep the flames from injuring the drivers before they can get out of the burning car.

racing team

Racing is a team sport. When you play football or basketball, you play on a team. Each person has a job to do. Racing is the same way. Yet many fans do not pay attention to the people on a racing team. They only want to see the driver. But the driver knows how important all the people on the team are.

Members of a racing team working on an engine (left) and brake system (right)

Here are some of the jobs on a racing team. Some people build engines for the cars. Some people clean and polish the cars and repair broken parts.

Changing tires during a pit stop at the Indianapolis 500

Some people change
the tires when they are
worn out. Some people
put fuel in the car.

Changing tires and
refueling happen when
the driver makes a pit
stop. The pit is the place

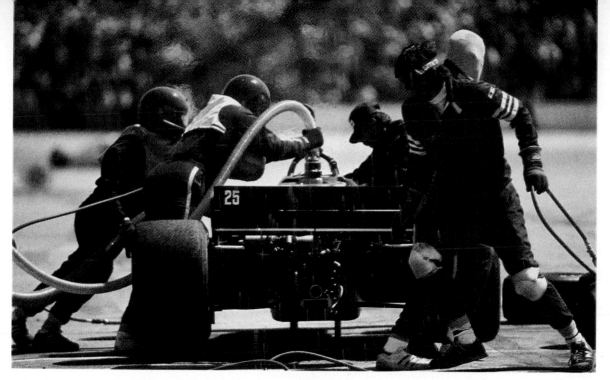

A fast pit crew is as important for winning a race as a fast driver is. A good pit crew should take about twenty seconds to change tires and refuel.

by the track where the driver drives when the car needs tires, fuel, or repairs. The people who do this are called the racing crew. Most drivers have also had practice being on racing crews.

racing crew

pit

Racing is expensive. That's why professional race car drivers need sponsors. The driver displays the sponsor's name on the car (right) and on clothing and other equipment.

Racing costs a lot of money. Drivers and teams must find sponsors to buy their cars and pay their salaries. Sponsors are often rich people who love racing. Sometimes the sponsor is a company that puts its name on cars to advertise a product.

Drivers and crew work hard during long races. Some races are so long that three drivers take turns driving.

Not all race drivers are young. Some are parents, even grandparents. In some

Racers Al Unser, Sr. (left) and Al Unser, Jr. (right),
also known as "Big Al" and "Little Al"

races, drivers race
against their own
children. Getting older
does not mean you
have to stop racing. You
can exercise and stay in

good condition. If you don't drive anymore, you can run a team or coach young drivers.

Racing drivers work all year. The racing season starts in January and is not over until Thanksgiving. The weeks between seasons are used for testing and working on the cars.

Some race car drivers become very famous and have large fan clubs. People collect their autographs. They get to travel back and forth across the United States every season. Sometimes they go to other countries.

There are many drivers in a race. Only one team gets to win. But when they win, all the hard work is worth it!

WORDS YOU SHOULD KNOW

autograph (AW • toe • graff)—a person's name, signed by hand

blowout (BLOH • out)—a hole blown in a weak spot in a tire

driver's license (DRY • verz LY • sens)—a card that permits a person to drive a car alone

fan club (FAN KLUB)—an organization of people who admire a famous person

go-kart (GO KART)—another name for "kart" (see below)

kart (KART)—the smallest race car. Its engine is like a lawnmower motor. Karts can be raced by eight-year-olds.

paved (PAYVD)—covered with a firm, level material for smooth driving

pit (PIT)—an area beside the race track where cars are repaired or refueled during a race

pit stop (PIT STOP)—a stop that a race car driver makes during a race to have the car refueled and repaired and the tires changed

race track (RAYSS TRAK)—a special road on which races are run

racing crew (RAY • sing KROO)—the people who work on a race car in the pit during a race

racing team (RAY • sing TEEM)—all the people who take care of a race car to help make it a winner

refuel (ree • FYOO • ul)—to fill a car up with gasoline

season (SEE • zun)—that part of the year when professional races take place, from January through Thanksgiving

sponsor (SPAHN • ser)—a person or company that pays for a race car, its repairs, and the salaries of the team and the driver

INDEX

PHOTO CREDITS

ABOUT THE AUTHOR

Sylvia Wilkinson was born in Durham, North Carolina, and studied at the University of North Carolina, Hollins College, and Stanford University. In addition to five novels, she has written two nonfiction books on auto racing, *The Stainless Steel Carrot* and *Dirt Tracks to Glory*; an adventure series on auto racing; Childrens Press's *World of Racing* series; and articles for *Sports Illustrated*, *Mademoiselle*, *Ingenue*, *The American Scholar*, *The Writer*, and others. She is currently a contributing editor for *Autoweek*.

Ms. Wilkinson is timer and scorer for Bobby Rahal's Truesports Indy racing team, Rinzler Motoracing, Clayton Cunningham Racing, and the Nissan prototype.